GW00763199

A T
For Reflection

(New Street - Ledbury)

Crazy Al Murray

Published by New Generation Publishing in 2014

Copyright © Crazy Al Murray 2006

First Edition

www.newgeneration-publishing.com

 New Generation Publishing

Dedication

There are so many people, events, places, artists, musicians
and circumstances that have inspired and affected my life
that it is an almost futile task to construct a suitably pithy
dedication. I am grateful for the gifts of my six senses - my
abilities to read, write, listen, smell, taste, touch, but most
of all, my intuition, There are two Muses that stand out
larger than life - Bob Dylan and my liver!!

To my ex-wife Katzy.

Acknowledgements

Were it not for my wonderful, late parents, James and Joyce, this wouldn't have happened - I thank them both deeply for their loving devotion to me and my siblings.

My sisters, Alison and Janet, and brother John, and their respective families - too many to mention by name. All of the great friends that I've made in a myriad of different places, especially Stuart "Dr. Clap" Hill, John and Mary Morris, John and Teresa Strike, and all of those patient souls who have offered me Shelter from the Storms.

My divine step-mother Marian, who accepted the Murray family with open arms when father and she got married in 1989.

So sad that father contracted cancer and died within 12 months of their most romantic respective second marriage.
Marian is a delightful, optimistic rock who it is a pleasure to have as an adopted mother - thank you Marian for giving all of the Murray family so much love and succour.

My three influential English teachers - the late George Sayer, friend of J.R.R.Tolkien, Alan "Sluice" Carter and Dougie "Drac" Mensforth - each inspirational in their own inimitable ways.

My long-suffering ex-wife Katzy, and my two fantastic children, James and Lorna - each of them bricks,but bricks with vision.

My glorious, gorgeous grandson George "Smiler" Green.

My lovely current partner Miriam without whose support over the last three years I would have been entertained permanently in one of those "One Flew Over the Cuckoo's Nest" hotels!

Lastly, to my two faithful patrons and benefactors Donald Richards and Jim Campbell who have patiently steered me down the right path if not the righteous!

Author~Bio

Born in 1956 in the beautiful rolling rurality of
Herefordshire - birth-town of John Masefield,
late poet Laureate. Son of a local, Scottish veterinary
surgeon, ornithologist and polymath. Educated in Malvern
and subsequently St. Andrew's University where he
degreed in English & Philosophy and carousing.
Worked in farming, game-keeping, scrap-metal and
finally I.T. He was a consultant with Cap Gemini
Ernst & Young for 10 years.
Interests include a passion for cricket, rugby, chess, films,
literature and wildlife. A cynical sceptic of history yet
inherently interested therein. Divorced with two children
aged 21 and 19.

Index

1............Foggy Ephemerality
2............Mad Dog Murray's Sexual Muddle Model
6............3 Men of Wisdom - The Magi
9............Bush and Blair
13..........Awe-fully Wonderful
14..........Enriched English - World Majesty
18..........Love-Fire
19..........Spooner's Word-Scrambling
20..........Strings-Free
22..........Pillocks of Society
24..........To Be Alone With Me (And You)
25..........Cyber-World
27..........Adam and Eve
28..........Song to Bobby Dylan
30..........Cracked Head
32..........Mournful Monday - Tale Of Movie Blue
36..........Moderation - Loves Not A Game
38..........Homelessness - An Epic Essay In S.O.S. Essence
42..........Shrub and Glare - Parabalic Converters
44..........Stags-Talking
46..........Your Smile
48..........Delirium-Free Men
49..........Etna's Eruption - Once More Unto The Beach...
52..........Headache
53..........Oak-Lore
56..........Self-Esteem
59..........Soulful Lady

Index

62..........Spring
64..........Unrequited Love
65..........When I was Young
69..........Wicca-Man
72..........The Milk of Humanity
74..........People are Strange
76..........Slave of Time
78..........A Ravenous Dream
79..........Sub-Dylanesque Blair-Sick Blues
82..........As I Recall
83..........Confusion's Confucius
85..........Our Don
86..........Our Don - Postscript
88..........Lorna, Lorna Lovely
90..........Lorna – Age 18
91..........My Son James

Foggy Ephemerality

Fog, fast-falling, envelopes noiselessly,
Sombre, but clearly sodden, bare bowers
Gone are those thicket files waved restlessly,
By incessant gusts and deep-struck showers,
Autumnal russet usurps summer green,
As trees are robbed of their mortal attires
The soft power of the warm-thronèd queen,
Succumbs to Winter's pleas and so, retires.

Can we outlive the eternal cycle?
Shall Winter's rebellion be strong opposed?
Our lives are yoked by a contract fatal,
Where evasion should rarely be supposed,
For, as certain as gliding fog descends,
So, all life, at death, ultimately ends.

Mad Dog Murray's Sexual Muddle Model

Martian men and Venusian women,
A thought to conjure with.
Only women can multi-task,
Now that's provocative!
As I read and pondered,
Simultaneously,
I disagreed with me and he,
Most philosophically.

I can multi-task, I must be female,
Heavy hammer, straight-striking nail!

Mad Dog I may be,
It's my prime degree.
But not because I'm a lunatic,
Or raving around and bent.
I'm just a household brick,
On brickly-vision intent.
If I'm now a lady,
I know it sounds quite crazy
I must be lesbian -
Don't fancy Bill or Dick,
Dave, Jim, Will, Les or Ian.
Then the penny dropped,
My confusion stopped,
The lock-key clicked.

An octagonal model sprang to mind,
Four nodes on the left, as men,
Four on the right – women.
(Canons to the left, tigers to the right!)
Representing outward sexual kind,
Dicks and tits, and other bits
That give the first impression.
Inward emotion,
And sexual orientation
To be detail more refined.

In its simplest state - four types,
Sorts of state of mind, if you like:
Hetero-he,
Hetero-she,
Homo-he,
Homo-she,
Each of these could co-exist, co-be
With either physical form,
He or she, you know, the norm(!?)
Each its own psyche,
e.g.
A multi-tasking, male-bodied, lady-lover,
Quite clearly
A he homo-she;
A single-threading, she-bodied, lady-lover,
Obviously
A she hetero-he.
Do you see?

3

The model formed quite elegantly,
Became, ipso facto, an entity.
Down the left I'd charted,
By the four octagon points
He - hetero-he,
He - homo-he,
He - hetero-she,
He - homo-she.
On the right I'd started
The mirrored counter-point,
She - hetero-he,
She - homo-he,
She - hetero-she,
She - homo-she,
The symmetry delighted me.
I hope you're all following me?

Then came the tricky bits,
How to present relationships.
Like a bolt it hit,
My psycho-gambit,
Join each and every point
With lines to signify
Why you, they and I,
Need a big fat joint!
So many possibilities,
For incompatibilities,
I found it really freaky.

Are you still with me
Dear patient ... Reader?
If not - then, maybe,
Sketch it out,
Erase all doubt,
You'll soon see
What struck me -
Freud and Gray no sentient leaders.
An astro-zodiac chart,
Not retro-maniac art.

Happy with this ingenious invention,
Breaking all known convention,
I sought a name to tag it,
Suitable to flag it,
For minds to bend, bounce, bewilder, boggle -
"Mad Dog Murray's Sexual Muddle Model"!

3 Men Of Wisdom - The Magi

Those three wise men of the orient,
The Magi as they're known,
Or were they three wise monkeys?
Hear no, speak no, see no.
With their strange gifts -
Armani gold - touch no,
Chanel myrrh - smell no,
Fabergé frankincense - no sense of taste.
Have you ever snuffed that sniff?!

Don't know about you,
But I wonder the significance
Of their presents,
Their stellar-guided reverence.
Melchior - a rep from ancient Christian Dior?
Kaspar - chess grand-master's great-great-great....
Grandfather?
Balshasar - the one who watched the star?
Mysterious names conjured
From who knows where?
Magicians' names.
Fabulously fantastic,
Such sagastic sojourns,
Their curious caravanserai.
Not a word of it relayed,
No bandit-raids,
No wolves, lions, mermaids,
Just their kingly cargo.
Speak no ...

What tongue did they use?
Or did they stand stone-mute,
Genuflect before the infant cute,
As shepherds blew their pipes and flutes?
So many master-painters scribed this scene -
"The Adoration of the Magi",
Supplicants in gold-lamé suits,
Clever cats in sky-rise hats,
Dumb-founded, awe-struck, bemused.
Speak no ...
See no ...

Could they comprehend words uttered?
Mary's, Joseph's, shepherds'?
Maybe no-one even muttered?
In amongst the barn-yard stench,
Camel, ox, ass, sheep and turds,
Those magicians knew what mattered.
The bray, the baa, the low,
Smell no ...
Hear no ...

Slurried straw-steam rising,
Mystifying the Holy scene,
Blurred by nativity tableau,
The masters made its pristine,
A venue fit for baptizing.
They should have realized though,
At Christmas you must book early
To avoid disappointment.

So, a reeking stable,
A manger for anointment,
Oats and hay for tea.
"Sorry - tea's off love."
Taste no ...

Did they play pass-the-baby?
Any goo-goos or coochy-coos?
Did he have his Mother's eyes?
Was his swaddling pink, or white, or navy?
Where was the humble farmer,
In that aromatic panorama?
Did the inn, "The Single Star",
Send them wine and victuals?
Ask them to play bar-skittles?
In that scene of Majesty
Were they all T.T.?
We'll never know!
Touch no ...

Bush and Blair

Bush and Blair, that unholy pair,
The puppet and the puppet's puppet,
Waging wars when oil is there,
Waldorf and Statler muppets.
They meet, they smile, do they care?
Saddam's gone, Mugabe rages on,
No human rights issues there!
Zion rules with missile and bomb,
The roadmap takes you to hell,
Suicide reprisals, martyrdom,
The West does its level best
To smear a terrorist smell.
Marionette strings are tugged,
The special relationship tightens,
The rancour of investment bankers.
After that meeting they hugged,
"Thanks for the million - see you in Brighton".
It's of this we all should be frightened.
Are the pullers of strings just chancres,
Ghoulish, ghostly yarn yankers,
Symbols of sordid collisions,
Mogul multi-national missions?
Does Bush say or do what he thinks?
Blair's neo-conservatism stinks,
New labour nothing but front.
Democracy, autocracy, hypocrisy,
Insincerity spinning a smirk of serenity.

Osama they continue to hunt,
Saddam they've banged in the slammer.
Muslims outraged - mounting enmity,
A deck of cards used as a stunt,
Nuts cracked with the military hammer,
The jokers of the pack still concealed.
To Moses a burning bush was revealed,
Paul the Persecutor saw the light,
Bush and Blair need fire of nuclear proportions.
The marriage of puppeteer extortion,
Will shatter midst this foolhardy fight.
Looming elections prompt fawning deflections,
Footling facts and statistics
Keep the proles at bay,
No room here for rejections.
Brownian motions - Mammon mystics,
Spinners of webs and deceptions.
Can you believe a word that they say?
Skin-flicks, snuff movies - kick against those pricks,
Rumsfeldian stranglings of the English language,
Occasional adage strewn in a sea of verbal sewage.
Corporate comfort assured,
Sound-bites and tax breaks,
Old world - new age,
Party donations ensured.
Ayatollahs and Sheiks
Poor little birds in a cage,

Pawns in a game of high stakes.
Cabalic puppet-string tweakers
Lurk in the murk of the stage,
Coiling and writhing like snakes.
Satanic bell-ringing speakers
Bolster the strong - bash the weaker.
Pontius Pilate and conscious pirates,
Searching for wars to wage.
Stealth, wealth, logo'd sneakers,
Nothing of substance to fire at.
Bush and Blair fret and fiddle,
Putin's caught in the middle,
Bill Gates purchased the Pearlies,
No ethics, no morals, just girlies.
Third world labour gets diddled,
Tobacco, cocaine, cockle-pickers,
Old World consumerism reigns,
Marxism's gone down the drain.
British nationalism, racial factionalism,
Bigotry and hatred remain.
"Ban the Bum" stickers
The sad and squalid refrain.
Bush and Blair, they're to blame,
Each in the other's knickers.
It's fame, shame and that glorious game,
Ronnie and Maggie the same.
Butchers, thieves, jokers and tricksters
Divorced from the blood and the stain,
Pandering puppets with rapacious brains,
Slavering shits, salacious not sane,
Do they shoulder the burden or blame?

Hutton reports and select committees,
Buttoned lips in court-room and city.
The shams, schemes and ruses,
Shattered dreams - bomb fuses.
The voice of a people unheard
In this theatre of the absurd.
Race, creed, colour shouldn't matter,
When you see kids' brains splattered
For the hate of a Jew or a Kurd.
Bush and Blair sit in their chairs,
Countries broken and shattered,
Economy jugglers sanctioning cash smugglers,
Power-crazed - mad as Hatters,
No thoughts for the poor old strugglers,
And behind the scenes
The string-pullers stay smug,
No sign of a twitch or a shrug,
Shades mask their eyes and their means.
Designer Beckhams, labels and jeans,
Don't rock the capitalist boat,
They sit back, laugh, then they gloat,
History will note - that they won with a vote.

Awe-fully Wonderful

I wonder what he thought as they pulled the ropes so taut?
I wonder - did he panic?
I wonder if he felt the pain as the lashes rained?
I did - it made me manic.
I wonder if they gave him a cheerful word or thought?
I worry that I witnessed it.
I wonder as they struck him - could he take that strain?
I'm sorry - I confess it.

I wonder if he smelt as they slashed his buckled belt?
I wonder - was he shameful?
I wonder if he felt the cold - stripped, stark, subdued?
I did - it made me blameful.
I wonder if he heard them laugh at those cards they dealt?
I regret - I could not move.
I wondered of their feelings - his back-whip marks so crude.
Neglect? Nothing could I prove.

I wonder what they thought as his slumping head got caught?
I wondered, why the hook?
I wonder if they felt his pain as it pierced that brain?
I did - I could barely take a look
I wonder if they knew who caused those thuds of thunder?
I wondered what words I'd said?
To this day I'm not sure the reason why I wonder ....

'Cos I'd shot those bastards ..... dead!

Enriched English - World Majesty

Angles, Saxons, Jutes,
Vikings too
Gave us little beauts,
Me and you.
Grot, grime and sod,
Slog, slime and plod,
Womb to woman,
To ask was acsian
Just arks a West Indian.

Greco-Latin's were quite able,
To confuse.
The polysyllable,
We oft' abuse:
Xenophonic paranoia,
Onomatopoeia,
Aquarium, vivarium,
Te deum, mausoleum,
Micro-wave, telesales,
We still use polymorphs today.

But the Bible - the good book,
There's a place to dig!
Ever take a look?
The names are often big,
Nebuchadnezzar - man with feast,
Shadrak, Meshak and Abed-nego,
The thousand and three degrees!
Babylon and Abyssinia - should we go?

Potiphar should have been a verb,
Preferred to potter, as in garden;
Gomorrah's much forgotten,
But Sodom's here to curb.

Then Franco-Normans,
Bretons too,
Gave a little romance
To our wordy zoo,
Beaulieu, dégringolade,
Fritillary, Marquis de Sade,
Beauty and kerosene,
Madame la guillotine.
Funny lot the frogs,
Stuff the goose and eat like hogs!

Italian standards came our way,
Artists' talk
No "calloo-callays",
Knew spoon from fork.
Pianissimo, fortissimo,
Chiaroscuro, relievo,
Pontormo, "I'd kiss him though!"
Leonardo, Michelangelo - go go … Bravo.
Romeo, Romeo ...
Guiseppe Verdi's also been,
So much better than Joe Green!

Now the creepy Krauts
Waged two wars,
Never kicked us out
They've left their saws ...
Schadenfreude, zugzwang,
Angst and ausgang -
Geordie twang that "gang".
"Auf weidersein pet",
Freud, Jung, and Hegel,
Kant, Goethe, Schlegel,
Brahms, Beethoven,
The list goes on and on,
And I haven't even started yet.

We've nicked a few off others,
All of the Indians,
Staki-panis and their brothers,
Aborigines, Caribbeans,
Even Micronesians.
Kedgeree and Cherokee,
Khaki, Dhobi, Balti,
Lacrosse, squaw, teepee,
Chapatti, roti, bindi bhajee,
Boomerang, didgeridoo,
Wallaby, kangaroo,
Chukkas and cups Calcutta'd,
Empire made by fuckers -
Back to Anglo-Saxon,
Cnut and Lars Ericsson.

Then there's the words we've borrowed.
Poets, singers,
Writers too are not without their horrors.
Bell-ringers,
Campanologists with rhythm,
Rhyming Rabby Burns
And his sleekit tim'rous mus,
Everywhere we've turned
To find those words of use.
Pharaohs with schisms,
Arcadian anachronisms.
Whirling dervish, grinling gibbons,
Charlatan, Zoltan Ribli,
Rodolfo's asymmetry,
Dactyls and spondees,
lambs and trochees,
No - that's Greek-ese
Just like trapeze.

Who on earth came up with palindrome?
Why the hell should we put up with microphone?
Words with double-meaning
Like gay, queen and creaming.
Word-corruptions like Featherstone-Haugh,
Doesn't rhyme with "off", it's pronounced Fanshaw!
Words like Margot where the T is silent,
And ingot and harlot where it's not.
Shaw had ghoti spelling fish,
He knew linguistic majesty,
It's morphing melds no travesty,
He effused in enriched English!

Love-Fire

The mottled sky's robbed of its spangled gape,
As the wispy clouds are swept, torn and rent
By the gnawing wind that is never spent.
Seed-heads tipsily trace; remnant of rape
From the mother-plant. While we lie prone-twinèd
Dreaming timeless trips in far-off places,
Striving to interrupt our embraces.
The cool gusty-breeze shoots its weapon spinèd.
Mingling as one, sure-set our braziered bond,
Now the flame is kindled, and blazes strong,
So blasting gales enrage it and prolong -
Defeated, drifting away, they abscond.
Mundane facts cannot explain our Love-Fire;
It ever lasts, even to the death-pyre.

Spooner's Word-Scrambling

If you blew up Napoleon Bonaparte,
Would that make him Napoleon blown apart?
If you mixed with the cash-rich,
Would that make you rash and kitsch?
If you won the Lotto with a Lucky Dip,
Would you attract girls with ducky lips?
If you are a Twit and blistered,
Would that make you bitter and twisted?
When Abbott met Costello,
Did they think it cost a lot mit botello?
If you are a bird-watcher,
Does that make you a word-botcher?
When you drank a beer at the Boar's Head,
Did you realize you'd end up in a whore's bed?
When you asked for the bitter-shandy,
Did you follow up with a shitter-bandy?
Later, when you went to the Friar Tuck,
Did you believe they'd try to....I think not?!
If you performed your cunning stunts,
Would you expect some stunning....not a jot?!
If you bought a stunt kite,
Did you imagine some...don't be a clot?!
When you met that pheasant-plucker,
Did you call her a pleasant...not a lot?!
If you had a square-cut punt,
Did you describe it as a pair...I hope not?!
When you met the driver of a whale-tanker,
Did you call him a tale....you dopey sot?!

Strings-Free

When you give,
Do you give strings-free?
As you live,
Do you live strings-free?
No resentments, jealousy, anger?
No sentiments or hidden agenda?
What it is to give and not want to receive,
Like a jolt in the heart, please believe
What it is to live true to yourself,
No judgments, control - soul-health.

When you walk,
Do you walk strings-free?
As you talk,
Do you talk strings-free?
Not bitten-tongued or pursen lipped?
What it is to walk and not need to run,
A freedom of spirit - no fear of the gun.
What it is to talk free and honest,
No fear of response, retort - that's best.

When you kiss,
Do you kiss strings-free?
When you miss,
Do you miss strings-free?
No expectations of mail or calls,
No missing that charity ball?

What it is to kiss and not regret,
Heart-warming memory to reflect.
What it is to miss and remember,
And recall that merry December.

When you cry,
Do you cry strings-free?
As you die,
Do you die strings-free?
No words-unsaid, no buried hatchets,
No guilts, no Bob Cratchets.
What it is to cry your own sweet tears,
Heart-sapping streams to share your fears.
What it is to die and know you're not alone,
'Cos, after all, you're stripped to stark soul and bone.

Pillocks of Society

With swaggering walk and self-important talk,
Charlatan brags, boastful bravado bluster,
The Pillocks of Society strut round like General Custer,
Gung-ho, gauche, grotesque - at nothing do they baulk.

They're holier than thou, they want it and they want it now,
Arrogant and rude, acting so brash and so shrewd,
They'd have you believe they never get screwed.
The Pillocks of Society know the whys, the wheres,
and the hows.

They know the cost of everything and the value of nothing.
Show them an etch and they'll call it a sketch,
Tell them its price, then they're impressed.
The Pillocks of Society think they're really something.

The Pillocks prattle loudly, swell their chests proudly,
Wear creased denims, designer shirts, black brogues;
To them the world's full of spongers, tinkers and rogues.
Unprincipled, callous, unsound, they hate the world
profoundly.

It's so hard for the Pillocks of Society,
Maintaining all those false airs and graces,
Desperately trying to prove they're not racists,
Never finding kind words or niceties.

They talk of exchange rates, often swap mates;
Sexist jokes they relate, 3rd world politics they debate.
The Pillocks of Society think they're the state,
Back-slap one another as their egos inflate.

If there's one thing that would truly please me,
Something that would make me laugh out loud,
It would be a vanity virus which inflicted that crowd,
As deadly as HIV for the Pillocks of Society.

Sad to say, come what may, they're here to stay,
The Pillocks of Society are virulent bacteria,
Vomiting venom and verbal diarrhœæ,
Mutating immunities to what stands in their way.

To Be Alone With Me
(And You)

There's something so soothing about my own company,
Just for a while, every day to deliberate,
To draw it all together, plan ahead, cogitate,
Reach a calmer karma and sensual symphony;
Like pottering in the garden with Mother Earth,
Her soul, and her fee-paying guests.
If I'm digging in the Autumn it's Robin redbreast,
Who's the cheekiest chappy above every other.
It's a chance to make different types of communion,
The bread of life, and something not to be idly missed,
Life is there to be absorbed by every sense - then kissed.
People think you're mad if you describe this
miraculous reunion.
What makes this miracle so sexually sensual,
Is sharing it with you, quietly, as usual.

Cyber-World

Pulling, tugging and compelling,
Winsome wit wafted o'er the waves.
Enigmatic, magnetical
Charms expressed in words - yet smelling,
Scented sensually in staves,
Prompting replies poetical.

Broken-winged, lonely, baleful bird,
Cooing out her hurt, harm and hate,
Pleading passion and compassion,
Her cryptic cries my blood it stirred.
I metamorphed ere 'twas too late,
Winged my words electric-fashioned.

No Angel Gabriel, just me,
Stroking her with listening ears,
Sounded out her still, silent voice,
Absalom's Achitophel, we ....
Staunched her sobs and glistening tears,
Became cyber lovers of choice.

On my sweet Eve of Saint Agnes,
Her pen oded a Grecian Urn
Transfixing imagination,
Relating such times of sadness,
Of how she would like us to burn,
Burn in passion's jubilation!

Responding in kind I her sent
Pieces of a mind, now hell-bent,
To dig deeper and not relent,
She unfurled her petals and scent,
Deflowered herself - yet decent,
She drew the honeyed bee's essence.

We buzzed and bloomed for hour on hour
Losing all sense of time's mission.
We teased each other's fantasies,
Caressed, kissed, grasped mighty powers.
Conveyed electric emissions,
We mimed to please, and did we please?!!

They peaked the pinnacle - perfect.
Achitophel's Absalom - me.
Drained, inflated, saturated,
Crisply coupled and still erect,
Delving dives, drifting dizzily,
Touch-free lives yet consummated.

Adam And Eve

You were the apple of my eye
On a tree of fountained knowledge,
Confidant, friend, star in the sky.
I was green, still in love's college,
Undergraduated, smitten.
Came the bursting of love's balloon,
With animosity bitten,
Illusions shattered all too soon.
Was I the Adam to your Eve?
Tempted, tested, asp-snared in scorn,
Apple tasted with no reprieve,
Eden-exiled, paradise-torn?
Try as I might, I can't deny,
You're still the apple of my eye.

Song To Bobby Dylan

Dum-da-da-dum-dum - anything but humdrum,
Ballad of a Thin Man - don't understand,
Blues Subterranean - poor little bum,
Where ev'rything scanned and nothing was planned,
No clues in titles like Blues of Tom Thumb,
Dangerous man in a lacklustre land.

Chorus
The joker, thief, magician too,
Wise words written to me and you.
Tangled stranglings in deep-thought blues,
I shall be freed so soon - spite can't rob me,
No-one can sing those tunes quite like Bobby.

Mercury music and lode-stone lyrics,
Screeching baritone to guitar-licked drones.
Ahead of the game, defied his mimics,
Plugged into sockets those proud microphones,
Screamed at the cynics' semantic antics,
Harp-blower's innocent flesh on the bones.

Bridge
He squawks and he barks, he shouts and he screams,
Man for all seasons in ev'ryone's dreams.

Chorus

Watchtowered princes, superhuman crew,
Word-showered lines cascading to rhyme.
Shifting our patterns 'fore even we knew
Hard rains were falling, floods of changing times.
Howlin' wind it blew, organ-grinder grew,
Growled of sins and crimes, washed-out bells they chimed.

Chorus

He squeaked, peaked and freaked, went to see the geek,
Wobbled off his bike, divorced his first wife,
Murmured mild and meek, never heard to speak
Bloody-tracked desires, slow-trained shots of life,
Burlesqued his empire, saved afore 'twas chic,
Self-composed skyline, got timed out of mine.

Bridge

Chorus

Thieving love he crooned, beneath the pale moon,
Brought things home marooned, freewheeled the highway,
Barked a creaky tune, shone his silver spoon,
Showed us he could stay, didn't need to pray,
Knocked on Heaven's door, couldn't go so soon,
Mercy's morning play kept him from the fray.

Chorus

There for all to see, frank philosophy,
Basement blonded Quinn took it on the chin,
Flagged down double-Es, that man called Tiny
Told us to begin, beware men too thin,
Those lean and hungry like Montgomery,
Burnin' coal pourin', scowly frowns, then grins.

Bridge

Chorus

29

Cracked Head

In the cantilevered cranium of opprobrium,
Whilst the cycling tricksters natterjack in euphoria
There's a clicking kernel, ticking, mad-hattered, chicken chum
Pecking, clucking sand-scratching search for sanitoria.

Sanity bones picked by the beaks of the hawks and the geeks,
Profanities droned in dastardly domes of the mental,
Devilish homes for society's freaks - they squawk, they shriek,
Lunacy's lurid lentils, pulse-puréed and punk parental.

Rented minds in thought-waltzers, vented spleens on
deafened ears,
Soul-searching seekers of asylum in the vacuumed world,
Sans eyes, sans ears, sans everything - anything but tears,
Tears for the voices within - fears for the flags still unfurled.

Infirm and flaunting, insane and vaunting, nuts, not normal,
Spooked by the horrors that are haunting,
web-snared in the mind,
Hammer-housed, horrified, haggardly hacked off the formal,
Committed to a house, defined, cracker-jacket confined.

Uncoordinated, unknown and eliminated,
From the world so sane, flushed down the drain of
mental garbage.
Anti-social stated, cremated ere yet created.
Parents blamed for your rantings, ravings and bilious rage.

Raging torrents of abuse catapulting your misuse.
Cataracts of catafalques, cascading with cosmic Celts,
No chance to strike a sanic truce or live a life of Truths,
Just leathered-lashes, belts, no thoughts for you,
or what you've felt.

Felled forests once stood majestic in floral finery.
They say you should, you would, you ought, you must,
you've been bought,
You've been bought, but you could, you could have thought
less irony,
Psycho-babbled, blue-blazed boloney, lobotomy-caught.

Caw-cawed and stealth-skewered by white-coated nurse and steward,
Condition-tagged, pigeon-holed, duck-lined at a gypsy fair,
Shot to smithereens, smelted, squashed, squelched, sent, see-sawed,
Floating with Faith's flotsam, jettisoned with jetsam –
YOU CARE.

Carelessly slung, tossed on the seas of despond –
you're still there,
There, but gone to the mind-librarians, sense-scrutineers,
Butcher-braining barbarians - bonker-bashers beware,
Aware, a rebel-roused pirate, marauding mutineer.

In here, the clear thought-foundry, phobia-factory,
Lucidity large-looms spot-lighting those lunatic tunes,
Yet you're the poacher, they're the keepers in this
doubt-hatchery.
"Quis custodiet ipsos custodes?"
Brains, brawn, buffoons?

Mournful Monday - Tale of Movie Blue

'Twas on a Monday morning,
Just like her school's first day,
Be happy, bright, not yawning.
Photo-shoot, big screen-play,
She'd replied to an advert,
Fresh out of acting school,
Classical, not dirty flirt,
Hoped not to play the fool.
Funny words they'd used - "virgins", "unabused",
"Fresh-faced fillies", to her they were not clues.

'Twas on a Monday morning,
To him another week
Of low-life, lurid porning,
Chic Afrique, tragic Greek?
Not a bit of it - just tits,
Up on cue, no "thank you"s.
Skin-flicked dicks with filthy skits,
"Swedish nudes", "Balls 'n Blues",
With his face unshorn, heart and soul hard-worn,
Forlorn with unborn sentiments of scorn.

'Twas on a Monday morning,
To her a sucking show;
Last night she'd been a-crawling,
Leg-loose and full of snow.

Coordinate these blind dates,
Is what she had to do.
Could not relate to her mates,
Never knew who they screwed,
Didn't query much - that was her, as such,
Drugs her only crutch, hated to be touched.

'Twas on a Monday midday,
To him his biggest win.
Girlie gay - they'll come what may,
Centre-spreads, Mickey-fins,
He was rotten through and through,
Cared for his family,
His friends, just like you and me,
Cash came so readily,
Loved his sordid life, ne'er told his darling wife,
Didn't recognize her struggles, strains or her strife.

'Twas on a Monday midday,
Her focus on their play.
"Close-ups pay" was what he'd say,
"Forget your fuzzy frame".
She felt finger flip to clip,
To catch the bump and grind,
Toe to hip and parted lips,
She tried to void her mind.
Her loss, not their gain, her down-beat refrain,
Visioned, Coltrane-brained, Vermeer and Verlaine.

'Twas on a Monday midday,
Desperate call to arms,
Stand-in stand-up was his trade,
"Hope this ain't a false alarm"
Red Adair's blue double,
Did films like "Animal Farm",
Dug them out of trouble,
Didn't give a hoot, ambled on the shoot,
"Who blows who? You look cute! –
d'ya like my suit?"

'Twas on a Monday tea-time,
Her eyes now opened wide,
Hadn't realized the grime,
She'd swallowed - not her pride.
In her hand a thousand bucks,
No Shakespeare anymore,
Moans and sucks in trailer-trucks,
"'Tis Pity She's a Whore",
"The Duchess of Malfi" and "White Devil",
She'd done them all, now she's on their level.

'Twas on a Monday tea-time,
He'd failed to come on cue.
Stand-up stand-in did the crime,
He'd said "We don't need you".
"Stick it where the sun don't shine,
I don't need you either
In my mind I'm more refined, a secret believer".
He upped, sought, went, morose and penitent,
Job more decent, soul-close and reticent.

'Twas on a Monday tea-time,
She un-packed her make-up,
Her mirror smeared white with rime,
Dealer'd called for take-up,
Purse unlocked - just round the block
She'd see her handy-man.
Looking at the wall-clock
She saw she'd missed that scam,
Into ex-actor she ran, slumped to floor,
"I can't stand no more, jab me at your door".

'Twas on a Monday dinner,
In a bar for sinners,
Boozer-losers, dream-winners,
Three-some of beginners,
Producer, Sec and Actor,
Spoke as though ne'er they'd met.
He'd sacked her to attract her,
Immersed in deep regrets
As they sipped their cokes, barman, softly spoken
"Each of you I'd choke, 'stime to quit your jokin'".

'Twas on a Monday midnight,
Lights were dim, "One Star Inn".
"Foresight, hindsight, insight,"
These three bright gifts we bring,
Sex and drugs and rock n' roll,
Here's a handle you can hold;
Forget the Queens and Kings,
Honest to your brother be, sister too,
Love yourself like them, kiss them all, please do.

Moderation - Love's Not A Game

To look not stare
To admire not scare
To smile not leer
To lure not fear
To warm not toast
To take enough not most
To hug not crush
To kiss not gush
To drink not drown
To respect not crown
To ease not shove
Not try to win in love

To be frank not blunt
To encourage not shunt
To agree not crawl
To be a clear not drawl
To persuade not rant
To stand not slant
To know not crow
To pass not throw
To talk not fight
To use peace not might
To be level not above
Not try to win in love

To grasp not snatch
To listen not catch
To coach not preach
To broach not breach

To discuss not argue
To attach not glue
To yield not grudge
To feel not judge
To laugh not sneer
To praise not jeer
To be hand in glove
And not try to win in love

Homelessness:
An Epic Essay In S.O.S. Essence

Shuffling down strange streets,
No sanctuary for mind or soul,
Noisily silent bars, cafés, greasy spoons,
"Sunset Strip", "Seven Stars",
"Smokin' Sam's", "Shalimar",
"Strangled Stork", "Cole's Law-less Store",
Only speak to tight-lipped, strait-laced staff,
So strenuous to stir a smirk or a laugh.

Shunned, cold-shouldered,
Ostracized,
Poverty-trapped,
Striving to sustain self-respect,
Suppressing depressing self-pity.
Starkness at sunset,
Solitary, soul-destroying sojourn,
Straining cerebral sinews.
Interview after bloody interview,
Just to see if the state,
Suggests some solace-asylum,
Or semblance of Social Security
For a citizen,
When all is sodding said and done!

Smoking cig on cig successively,
Shifting suit-case from semi to slum,
Starting a slippery slide,
A slither down the maelstrom,
Spinning round and around.
Cynical, snarling, sarcastic,
Sitting snuggly, like spy-spotters,
Spitting smugly with fly-swatters,
They say "So you seek assistance?
Surely you sense there's strict constraints?
You're no Slavic, Somali or Saint!"
They hiss as they pronounce those sibilants.
You're stunned, gob-smacked, de-sensitized,
As you stare into their stark eyes -
"But I assumed..."
Sentence bisected -
"You know what assume does?
It makes an ASS out of U and ME!"
Hiss-hiss-hiss-he-he.
Satanist soul-snatchers
I spew on your stupidity,
I scream, scratch, scrape, stab,
Subliminally, of course
"So suggest something" I say.
"Sod you - next please".

So homelessness is not so simply sorted!
Signs of something smelly in the social perspective.
Someone said six seasons gone - "Sky-rise styes sordid,
Swamps for swine, stinking, squalid, septic".
A sense of symbolic simplicity smacked me suddenly,
A special, inspirational story - not history -
Sparked serenity and bliss - it's this...

Seven sycophants spent seven summers sailing.
"So" said" simple Simon, "something special shall stir us."
"Minestrone soup's for stirring" said stoic Steve.
"Strogonov for supper" slinked Slovenian Styrus.
"Syllabub for sweet?" sultry Samantha pleaded.
"Semolina also" Selina softly sneered.
Steph suggested "Sauterne to slosh it sunder."
Sex-Free, supping cider, stuck stolidly
at the stern and steered.

"'Snot that" said Simon,
" 'Tis something else supports our scheme.
Cast your nets on t'other side, special species
swim submerged,
Sumptuous catch we'll snatch.
Saints, solicitors, Samaritans, All Souls, clickety-clicks,
Satan's there also, slavering,
Squirming, slithering, snake-smoothly stammering
six-six-six.

On the seventh day, of the seventh week,
of the seventh year,
At the seventh hour - now, it's here -
Seventy-seven sinners shall be saved.
So seventy surplus soles seek us."
As they cast their nets o'erside,
This sturdy skiff capsized.
Seven sycophants a-swimming
Amongst a sea of seventy shoalless souls!

The sting of this essay on essence
Is: "Say One's Esses,"
Or is it "Save Our Shoals?

Shrub & Glare - Parabalic Converters

Madam was a cow-car-girl - she simonized her Ford,
Just a rough 'n ready model, late sixties Capri.
She'd paid ready money, it was all she could afford.
Loved that car above all else, including family.

Shrub lived over the river, drove a new white Rolls-Royce,
He didn't give a toss, because he had a chauffeur
Whose name was Glare, he'd gloss, he'd care,
for he had no choice,
Whate'er Shrub said, Glare went and did, didn't dare demur.

One day Shrub's Roller got bashed, he didn't know
by whom,
He thought it was a hoodlum known as Mad Sin-Laden,
No reason why he took this view, prejudice assumed.
Glare and Shrub went hunting, as if for some fair maiden.

Sin-Laden, elusive fox was he, no hide nor hair,
Could they trace - his near-neighbours bore bold
brutal brunts
Of unsolicited assaults, intrusions - no one there.
They sought high then higher, all was backed on
these hunts.

The neighbours gave up - said "He ain't here,
he's a mere pup."
Shrub turned on Madam - asked if she'd lend him her motor.
She didn't like his touch, or him that much, asked
"What's up?"
Said Shrub "Miss, if ya don't give me this, I'll use voters!"

42

Glare argued with Shrub for using United Notions' stance,
Said "See sir, on the Tower of Babel, all is square,
We've got a Court of Uncivil Wrongs by sheer happen-chance."
"Get thee behind me" said Shrub, "you're not all there, young Glare."

Without further ado they'd raised a posse anew.
Poor Madam, her kith and her kin were haunted like knaves.
They hadn't a prayer 'cos her Ford was good as new.
They banged up Madam, her neighbours they treated like slaves.

At this point in time things went from the daft to sublime,
Madam's Ford Capri dissolved into meaningless slime,
Sin-Laden, for he, was called to Vatican Court
Where Pope said "Don't bugger your neighbour - my final thought."

Stags-Talking

Steaming breathed stag amongst battered, browned bracken,
Snorting, dribbling, foam-frothing from frenzied mouth.
No cuckold - no wall-flower as you sniffed her,
Stinking, stonking, sexy harem-sentinel,
Slavering, licker-tongued tail-lifter,
Nosing the air, sucking, gulping smells –
I see your groinal swell.

I look, I dream
I'm not one of these,
I look, I scream
I love to, to please.

He's soul-proud, antler-envied, Bacchic, Minotaur-mad,
Mad for her, and her and her - ye desperate,
demented drooler,
Steamed-cruiser, serial carouser, mantled in the crown of
Both shimmering and withered kings, and Tyson-tigered
In sinews tautened, Boris Karloff'd,
Horned, hewn, toned and hunked, primed to give her
What she wants - a poker-stork her wishes - so, so bad.

I look, I dream
I am one of these
A stag supreme
Statuesque, at ease.

Oh ye panting, lick-lusted, musty, "love's the life," Lothario -
Come to me darling, you're more than a disco-tagged hind,
d'ya mind?

A before that's thereafter, or another notched behind.
You ooze those sweet, slurped, scented juices,
apple-sucklinged,
Lugubriously labial-swelled, resined cedar tree,
Aromatic box of delights, honey-potted, primed for me.
Not a target on a board, or someone else's wife,
The stag, he claims and spunks his territory,
he humps, then strikes.

I look, I dream
Am I one of these?
In creaming jeans,
Dark desires unfreezed?

The rutting, barking, butting, bravado'd bluster,
Quickified, cock-satisfied, fumy-fired fluster.
The hinds on heat take his hornèd hugeness, his meat.
Coital roars, bilging, "You're all dead Custers,
Stuck up there, on that hill, that hill of Death."
He gives them sweaty, steamy shags so sweet,
Sweet hinds, a shag to remember, to savour, to lustre.

I dream, I look
One of these I am,
Another book,
Pleasing where I can.

Your Smile

Your smile inspires a sun-kissed morn,
Courting doves strutting and preening,
Happy with life, glad to be born,
A world of form, beauty, meaning,
Your smile's a present wrapper torn
Revealing a gift of heart and feeling.

Your smile's the smile of a rose in bloom,
Fragrant, bright, and oozing grace,
A sign of something coming soon,
A God-blessed star-burst 'cross your face,
A Jacob's ladder to the whitest moon,
Your smile's white satin on sheer black lace.

Keep on smiling and keep on flying,
Light up the world to stop it crying.

Your smile delights whoever's near,
It radiates with fun and passion,
The finest wine and the coolest beer,
Sexier than the smoothest fashion,
To all around it brings great cheer,
Black derby hat with white trimmed sash on.

Your smile is like a lake so clear
Inviting guests and skinny-swimmers,
Far deep and dark and yet so near,
Back-hair shivers and goose-bump shimmers,
Titian, Rubens and Jan Vermeer,
Your smile gives hope a gleeful glimmer.

Keep on smiling and keep on grinning,
Light up the world to keep it spinning.

Your smile could launch a million ships,
They'd slide out to sea without a shove.
A song of praise framed in luscious lips,
Heaven-sent like the stars above
Your smile has got me in its grips,
It's etched in ivory, honed with love.

Keep on smiling and keep on beaming,
Light up the world to keep it dreaming.

Delirium-Free Men

Mind-loose, head-sore, cold grot-gravy glum,
Money-poor, leaden-goose, got no navy rum,
Thought-jumping, heart-pumping, so I'm really shaky,
Short-fused, confused, prospects pretty flaky.

Eyes-blind, flat-broke, wrote a book today,
"Fat bloke, flies behind, the one that got away."
Stone-faced, bone-traced, in the cemetery,
Race-rattled, mace-battled, awful symmetry.
Strait-laced, double spaced, sunk without a trace,
Editor, predator, threw it out the double-door.
Creditors, creditors, just want more and more.

Upright, uptight, mutually inclusive,
Downright, midnight, tried to be illusive.
Common-sense, double-talk, in a world of spin,
Bubble-bath and incense to salve the pains we're in.

Blind-stoned, fly-blown, victims of an outrage,
Pig-sty, bacon-rind, pink gins on centre stage,
Steak n' Chips and Big Macs, mean nothing to those folk,
Battle-ships, chips in stacks, a poker-gaming joke,
War-torn, forlorn, they hunt new lives to lead,
Forewarn the unborn, for they're the lambs who'll bleed.

Cool-blooded, diamond-studded, power-crazed, unsullied,
Blood-money, stud-honey, flower-dazed, not worried,
Mad-bannered, bad-mannered, shower-glazed in slurry,
Star-spangled, spar-strangled, towers razed, not quarried!

Etna's Eruption
(Once More Unto The Beach...)

Ominous beside the orange orbèd sun,
The billowing belches of sulphurous fumes
Threatening the inevitable emission,
Etna stands as the Damoclean looms
With all passion in suspension.

Dormant, and yet imminently explosive,
Like a slumbering soulless Cyclops,
At times beckoningly permissive,
To our gaping gazes at its shy tops
With never a hint of heightened bliss if...

Only a matter of time before blossoms,
Will shred the calm spitefully asunder,
Coughing, choking, churning cloud-tantrums;
Gore-groans and more moans before thunder
Cracks and splits the air with cruelsome
Searing screams silencing all above and under.

At last, at last,
Milk-thick lava
Steaming as it flows;
Slow then fast,
Heavenly dew, a
Dribble down the rose.
An asp aghast
Oozing downward
Hissing as he slows.

Up and up, and down
Spits the mount
Aiming at, who knows?
Smother and drown -
The fitful fount
Shoots its airborne arrows.
Flamed eider-down,
A warlock's bounty,
Suffering prickling pillows.

The dam has burst
And now it leaks,
Weeping down below;
It taunts the cursed,
Kills the weak,
And shimmers as a willow.
It does its worst,
Sprays the meek
And falters those that know.

All is swept aside before the flowing gush,
None can stem the torpid tide
Winding onward with every ebb and rush,
Masking some mighty pump astride
The seatless source of all that's lush.

The bucks and quakes begin to lapse,
Those spasms of mortal death-twitches,
As heaven reclaims those vital saps
And earth retains her breath's riches
Before its exhalation, and collapse.

Etna puffs and pants in solitude,
Her structure reclines once more,
Serenely silent in an attitude
Of ecstatic exhausted ardour;
A suspended catalyst, and food
To the echo of her deafening roar.

Headache

if you're stumbling about
with your head on a stick
if you bite at the world
when you just need to lick
if your overglazed ears
are about to implode
from the grating of gears
for the next episode

if the trumpeting mouths
and the fingernail screams
of this tubular dream
squeeze your cheeks til it seems
that you can't feel the sides
of your life through the glare
while the taste of your days
is too acid to bear.....

and Alka-Seltzer doesn't help much either

Oak-lore

A huge hunk of wood am I,
Four hundred years or more I've idled my while,
Stained, twisted and grooved,
But by the stresses of time,
I remain completely unmoved.
I once was the rudder of an ocean vessel,
Turning and straining 'gainst the surfing seas.
I saw battle with pirates and Spaniards,
Hawsers, painters and lanyards,
Cutlass, canon and grape-shot,
Landlubbers, seamen and soldiers,
All are long-distant, murky memories.
Hewn from the bough of a Surrey oak,
That had stood in the forests for centuries:
From acorn to tree to ship-yard,
From ship-yard to sea to scrap-yard
And thence to the builder's spoke-shave.
Now a pivotal prop in the old Plough,
So much has changed from then 'til now:
Gone is the saw-dust floor,
Gone is the stable-door.
Synthetic memorabilia pinned to the walls,
Quasi-vintage sepia photographs,
Corn dollies, wooden tools, beer mats;
No backy-chewing, tonsil-tickling laughs,
Just the ping of the computerized till,
The whirr and zing of the fruit-machine,
As I lie across the unused chimney-breast,
An experienced eye of the unhearing world.

I've seen them come and noted their drill,
In this church of the mutating congregation,
In this world of rotating domination,
It's all a game now - nothing's a thrill.
The high swells bucked me,
The big swells suck see,
Now I've absorbed the vernacular,
I've lost my roots, but I'm still here,
Horizontal, astute, not perpendicular.
I've seen them come and go,
Some of them speak of Michelangelo,
Some of them talk of bits and bytes,
None of them know wrong from right.
My perspective of life is oblique,
I'm a veg after all, not Freud,
Nevertheless they're not all blessed,
Some have never confessed
That the world is one to avoid.
I've heard heated heart-aches,
Discussions and mass debates,
I've seen fights, feuds and fracas,
Flailing fists on wrought-iron wrists,
Little change from sea-faring days.
There have been bar-maid captains
Steering the inn-keeper's ship;
I've seen lily-livered landlord lieutenants,
They come and they go, and none of them know
The scheming, sanguine assassins,
Who would split a tongue and lip
Just to exact some miserly penance.

So nothing much changes - heigh ho!

54

Man's such a predictable pest,
Who eats, shits, loves and lives,
Caring little for all the rest.
We who remember forgive,
Seldom are we ever consulted,
The lingo's a problem I believe.
When I advise they're insulted,
Slam my cousin and hastily leave.
Yet every year they get back to their roots,
With the holly, the ivy and mistletoe,
Symbols of that time long ago,
When mutual motherly respect
Prevailed - not neglect,
Of life's inter-dependencies,
Awareness of earthly tenancies,
Antecedence, parental respect;
They knew, and we know the synergy,
Pollarding preserving energy,
Fostering forestry furtherance,
Flora and fauna flourishing
Unlike contemporary pillage,
Chopped, hewn, drilled and screwed,
Leaving a forest-scape all but nude.
I bide my time here over the hearth,
Hoping that values will change,
I encourage myself with a laugh,
Once they're gone they're just bones,
Burnt or buried under-earth,
Whilst I observe all alone,
Striving to conceal my mirth.
Time will come once again,
When Mother Nature's wheel
Will vanquish and reign,
And me? I'll just be part of a keel.

Self-esteem

When you are so low on self-esteem,
That you can't smile at yourself in the mirror,
And you feel like a horrible has-been,
The thoughts of an affair give you the horrors,
Pinch yourself 'til it really hurts,
And remind yourself that it's great to flirt.

If you're lying alone there in bed
Full of dread of facing the world,
Imagine yourself proudly strutting instead,
Like a Tom-cat, black, arrogant, uncurled.
A flashy fluorescent flag unfurled,
The sexiest man or the most gorgeous girl.

If you live with a large ear for the bad,
And the tiniest ear for the good,
Recall what it is to be happy and glad,
Think of the smell of a coniferous wood,
Deeply inhale that resinous fume,
From the depths of your memories your senses exhume.

Remember your six senses,
Don't dwell on your negative thoughts,
Present, past and future tenses.
It's not all just crosses and noughts,
There are also croughts and nosses;
Don't treat them like frivolous flosses.

Direct your thoughts to the taste of a view,
To the smell of a sound, the view of a touch,
Your psyche's the hub, your senses the purlieu.
Don't let the negatives become your crutch -
You are "a thing of beauty and a joy forever,"
Keats would never have said "Never".

Truly the world, and everyone in it, is your oyster,
There to be coaxed, caressed and canoodled.
You don't have to be extrovert to roister.
You don't need to be sexy to be poodled.
It's all an aura of being,
When all your senses are seeing.

Try to become "close bosom-friend" of the sun,
Imagine that you're no longer on the run.
What fun it is to grasp a conundrum!
What excitement to beat the humdrum!
You are physically oozing and radiating
Your sheer happiness is emanating.

Your mood and manner are infectious.
When you feel and act down and out
It hits your companions in the solar plexus.
When you're up, happy and smiling - there's no doubt,
Just like a magnet with iron filings
It's one up, all up, with the roof tilings.

Look into the mirror-happy to see, smell and touch me -
There are your ivory teeth, your laughter lines,
You could even fall in love with me,
Flooding back come all those happy times,
Accentuating the positive and walking on a brighter side,
Are just bound to turn the downside tide.

If the negative thoughts can get on top of you,
So can the positive - and you can put them there
if you dare.
You can gild the lily, smear rust with ormolu,
Whichever god you follow he or she really cares.
Verdigris some copper, fine-tune that chopper,
Become a vibrant vixen, venomous body-shopper.

The self-esteem lesson's a hard one to learn
RZ has it right - "don't follow leaders".
Be true to yourself - self-praise is the hardest to yearn,
Yet it's the most satisfying of self-feeders,
It puts you on the map and removes loads of crap,
And in place all those Lego pieces'll snap.

Self-esteem follows on from self-direction,
Give a big ear to your positive thoughts,
Let them be giant erections,
To the negatives give a string of noughts.
You have the power of ultimate selection,
To the negative you have the right and power for rejection.

Soulful Lady

You sat there crying in distress,
All alone with a stolen mind,
That cryptic painting loomed above,
Your soul screamed out "I need some love,
Please talk to me and treat me kind."
I talked to you - admired your dress,
Your ebony-skinned loveliness.

"Ever shot pool and had a laugh?"
"What's that painter trying to show?"
"Forget your troubles just chill out."
Your warmth shone through, I had no doubts.
"This is a man you'd like to know."
You talked of lion, ape, giraffe;
Magnetised with your vital spark.

Tearful baby cried at me
Sultry sugar dried by me
Soulful lady smiled for me
Hothouse honey sighed with me

Captured by your natural charm,
We talked of boats and planes and slaves.
I tried to beat the handsome man,
Kissed your cheek, and it all began.
Spoke of life's beauty, Daddy's grave,
Wept some tears, became becalmed,
Touched thighs and hands without alarm.

I wanted you but you weren't sure,
He played an open game of lust,
I asked you if you'd got a friend,
You said you'd have some time to spend,
Had had enough of soup and crust,
Your dark eyes flashed with signs impure,
For my injured heart it craved a cure.

Tearful baby cried at me
Sultry sugar dried by me
Soulful lady smiled for me
Hothouse honey sighed with me

We found a place to crash that night,
We played a game of cat and mouse,
He pushed his throttle to the floor,
Took you up to his bedroom door,
Dropped an ace to take the house.
You came back down to my delight
I knew right then twould end alright.

Come to me honey, please don't come,
Burn some money, forget discrete,
Remember to regret tomorrow,
Juice my yearning, soothe my sorrow,
Another day's a new clean sheet.
Blow that hunting horn, bang your drum,
Come to me honey, please don't come.

Tearful baby cried at me
Sultry sugar dried by me
Soulful lady smiled for me
Hothouse honey sighed with me

Panting breath on the nape of my neck,
Legs twined in the shape of a snake,
Smooth skin tingling to the softest touch,
I wanted your heart, oh so much.
Heart pumped 'til I thought it might break,
Dealt a card from a brand new deck,
Held her hand, for a final check.

Come to me honey, come once again,
Once the fire's kindled it burns strong
With a heat that's surely hellish,
A passionate flame to relish,
In the grips of a night so long,
Thunder, lightning, then soothing rain,
Come to me honey, come once again.

Tearful baby cried at me
Sultry sugar dried by me
Soulful lady smiled for me
Hothouse honey sighed with me

Spring

The spring bursts forth with floral-faunal energy,
Haggard, wizened trees making up,
First with foundation palettes of greens,
Then their blushers of blossomed exuberance.

Lengthening days luring avine arias,
Chorus, chirrup, unrestrained delight.
Doves strutting and nodding with lovers' persistence,
Tits flitting from branch to branch,
Butterflies flutter from plant to plant,
Wafting their peacock wings in sparkling Spring sun.

Laburnums cascading yellows,
Wisteria waterfalling lilacs,
Lilacs rocketing sensuous scents,
All of it Heaven sent.

Daisies, buttercups, dandelions,
The capricious cornucopia of colours
Erupting to the gardener's gleeful disgust.
Hedge-trimmings, lawn-clippings,
Aromas of life cropped in Spring.
Sweet, sweet the smells flitter and bust.
The pall of the car, the lorry and train,
Magical murder by the brawn and the brain.

Scents, sounds, horses, hounds,
Luscious lightings of delicious sightings.
Titianesque colours ablaze, nuptial sky-nightings,
Crazy moth burlesques piercing lunar luminescence.
All too soon the frantic frenzy of birth and awakening,
The bees' buzz and the hum become hum-drum.
Spring cedes to the burning Summer sun,
Fresh gloss colours fade into matts,
No sheen anymore, not clean, besmirched.
Fallen fledglings captured by cats,
Spent blossoms from Camellias, Azaleas and Birch,
Motifs, mottos, mausolea and grottos,
Cemeteries, carcasses, cadavers, and corpses,
The death of the Spring is a chastening thing.
Our hope is eternal cycles like these,
Knowing Autumn's death sickle
Inspires another make-up palette to please,
Tucked up leaves, leaf-lifts and browns.

Fresh-made tree-dresses and street-gowns,
The scrunch of the cast-offs make your ears tickle,
The scrape of the rake aches your knees.

Next Spring the bulbs'll burst through,
First-life after Winter's recession.

Unrequited Love

I sit here so contentedly
Watching your radiance
Bob slowly in the gentle breeze,
Your torso slender as a model's
Bending back and forth,
And limbs wafting sympathetically.

Delicate your aromas,
Subtler than a coffee-shop,
Less sickly than confectionary,
Less pungent than a swimming pool,
Simple, sweet and heaven-sent.

It's so sad that you are dumb to me,
Or is it that I don't listen?
Oh how I'd love to pluck you,
But you're better where you are.

Your head, your body, your essence,
I'd love to clasp thee to my breast,
I yearn to freeze you in suspension,
But I know that it can't happen
You can't return my love,
Or adoration.

I sit here so contentedly
Tears of admiration cheek-streaming
For soon you will be gone.
I wave to you and bid farewell .....
Floral beauties don't last long.

When I Was Young

When I was young I wasn't sure I was solid,
Through T.V. cartoons and other stuff squalid,
How could I prove I'm no 'toon creation,
Some celluloid victim with no destination,
Or a trash-mag Jock with strange fascination?
Now we're vacuum-packed, Tesco'd and trollied.

Through lasting and costly education
I began to learn my station.
When pricked I surely bled,
When kicked I often fled,
When tricked I frequently said,
"It's not fair - it's abomination!"

When I was young things were simple and clear,
Some things were far, others so near.
In the shops you were well-known
'Cos in your town you'd been grown,
Nurtured, fostered and shown
That Mother was dear and Father austere.

Well, my sisters, cousins and brother
Weren't like them or the others,
They did things more fantastic,
Didn't seem flat or plastic,
Never used words like zombie and spastic,
Had great friends, uncles and lovers.

Animal farm was our home,
Compassion was something we were shown,
Death to those old and infirm,
Was a sad fact we had to learn.
No squint, wince or squirm,
At that putrid body fly-blown.

The Beatles and Stones were a rage,
Bob Dylan rattled their cage.
On an old Bush machine,
With a pre-load magazine,
We'd dance to the sounds and preen,
No need for a screen or stage.

Lennon was cool, not Mick Jagger.
We'd squabble, drink and stagger.
Dylan's the man I'd hasten to add,
Inspirational, banal, even sad,
Not mainstream at all - I was glad.
So I walked like the others, with a swagger.

When I was young it snowed and stayed,
We had trays and sledges, so we played,
When it melted it caused great dismay,
Too moist to play cricket or footie,
Too few to play rugged rugby.
For sun, linseed and blanco we prayed.

JFK got shot - we watched on the box,
Dad called it the wireless - bless his woolly socks.
I couldn't care for Opportunity Knocks,
Hughie Green, the talking machine,
Monkhouse, the Shot, with his teeth so clean,
Ridiculous rubbish, some humour, no shocks.

Smith's salt and shakes were the thing.
Perry on Sundays with a napkin ring.
Trousers tied up with bailer string.
Stinky silage, Dinky cars, kinky boots,
Those winkle-picker shoes gave me the hoots.
I wanted to smoke, play piano and sing.

I wished I could bat like Sobers, drink and not fall over,
Pull some bird and roll in the clover,
Drive a car, maybe a Rover.
Happy dreams and high aspirations,
Pre-teen thoughts - flashed inspiration,
Who, after all were John and Jehova?

Minis, lip-gloss, hot pants and bras,
Electric guitars, motor-bikes, cars,
Skies full of stars, tad-poles, jam-jars,
Testosterone bubbling and boiling.
Lee Harvey from that bullet recoiling.
A world of daring dreams, creeps and stars.

I can see it still, I can smell the thrill,
I can hear the juke-box so shrill
That pumped and jumped down at The Drill.
Mods, rockers, donkies and crombies,
Lads riding round on combies,
Then I'd unhook a fish through a gill.

When I was young my time was my own,
Not like now that I've grown,
It's all deadlines, e-mails, mobile phones.
The light programme gave us the Goons,
Forces favourites and Uncle Mac's kiddy tunes,
Aunty Beeb had Steptoe's rags and bones.

If I'd known then what might unfold
I'd have paid more heed to what I was told,
By those fuddy folk who all seemed so old.
The waft of fresh mint, the tortoiseshell's tint,
Dragonflies glint with that shimmering hint.
When I was young I was bold, I never felt cold.

There were times like those, not these,
When everything was there to please,
It didn't matter when they tried to tease.
Life was a joy, ephemeral, a thrill.
I recall so well that strutting mandrill,
Circus lions, Coco clowns, the trapeze.

When I was young there was nothing morose,
That was an emotion that belonged to those,
Those who wore cravat, suit and a rose.
They cried at hatchings, matchings and despatchings,
They sobbed at everythings, nothings and somethings,
The scent on the wind, but not what it blows.

When I was young, I was young,
Now that I'm old, I'm still young,
Waiting for that song to be sung,
In which age, youth and beauty entwine,
No more pearls before swine,
No death-knell chimes to be rung.

Wicca-Man

Oh weird Wicca-man please sing me moon-tunes,
That tell me of life's pre-Christen-doom days,
Sprite's spirited songs, rhapsodic loon-runes,
Sabbatical spells and mystery plays.

The Holly, the Ivy, the Mistletoe,
Emblems and signs of a world long ago.
I'm a lucky man - I'm telling you so -
As sure as I'm here, I remember then,
Was Wicca a friend, not a means to an end,
Earth-man and Soul-Sun, a magical blend?

Camomile lotions, mystical potions,
Lunar devotions firing emotions
Forgot in today's cover-up oceans.
It's worse than you think - our history reeks -
The plight of women, who were smeared as freaks.
The Romans had gods, and so did the Greeks.

BRIDGE
Alive to Nature, at one, immature.
Druidical dances with virgins so pure.

CHORUS
Oh weird Wicca-man please sing me moon-tunes
That tell me of life's pre-Christen-doom days,
Sprite's spirited songs, rhapsodic loon-runes,
Sabbatical spells and mystery plays.

That Inquisition - she-persecution,
Wicca's position - bleak resolution,
Herod's massacre - God's revolution?
We lived and survived, to spite blinded eyes,
Our icons despised, witches stigmatised,
Tortures devised to stitch sage and wise.

But Wicca shall win - she'll withstand their spin,
She's not such a sin - I stand here and grin,
She began before the word was begin.
Wicca vanquishes 'gainst worldly wishes
She doesn't languish in vales of anguish,
Serves you fine dishes and tales like this is.

BRIDGE
Alive to nature, at one, immature.
Druidical dances with virgins so pure.

CHORUS
Oh weird Wicca-man please sing me moon-tunes,
That tell me of life's pre-Christen-doom days,
Sprite's spirited songs, rhapsodic loon-runes,
Sabbatical spells and mystery plays.

Moon is your Mother, as Sun's your Brother,
Some have it other, don't mind or bother.
Trapped by earthly dreams - look, there's another!
Where Wicca's crowned Queen, who rules hearts so clean,
Fairy-folk unseen - foolish farts obscene,
She's a whore, has-been - "no she's not" I scream.

Maya and Inca, Aztec, Zulu too,
Each have their relics, her happy voodoo.
I'm telling you now - believe that it's true!
To you I show things - you think that they're tricks,
With one of your rings - you're hale or you're sick -
Some say it's magic - doubting it's tragic.

70

BRIDGE
Alive to Nature, at one, immature.
Druidical dances with virgins so pure.

CHORUS
Oh weird Wicca-man please sing me moon-tunes,
That tell me of life's pre-Christen-doom days
Sprite's spirited songs, rhapsodic loon-runes,
Sabbatical spells and mystery plays.

I could weave you spells to aid harmony,
Mix some smouldrin' smells, inspire symphony,
All for Mother N's yin, yan 'n yoni,
But you've lost the thread - mammon's there instead,
To he you've been wed, you've been juiced and bled,
It's a tale unsaid - Wicca-man's undead!!

Propagandist Gandhi - whose heart's so missed -
King's killer off-pissed me - those dreams I kissed,
Lennon's on the list - Jesus too - long list!
Each was Wicca-wise, it's there in their eyes.
Those prayers I deny, not much applies,
You slayers I defy, my powers'll surprise.

BRIDGE
Alive to Nature, at one, immature.
Druidical dances with virgins so pure.

CHORUS
Oh weird Wicca-man please sing me moon-tunes,
That tell me of life's pre-Christen-doom days,
Sprite's spirited songs, rhapsodic loon-runes,
Sabbatical spells and mystery plays.

The Milk Of Humanity

Filtering streaks of sun, the life-giver,
Spot-lighting part through leaf-laden branches,
Twinkled starry sparks on th'unknown river.
Symphonic surging with sky-born blanches,
Like a perfect play, or faultless sliver
From favourite dreams, inspiring trances...

My shuffling steps split grass, till now untrod,
Leaving trenches through this virgin carpet,
Remnant of hostile feet, strangely shod.
Surrounded by a verdure amulet,
The water's lap seems safe from th'armed clod
Housing human hosts on destruction set.

Knee-deep in the blustering surge, still, I stand;
My naked frame devoid of civil proof.
The constant flow tugging with often bland,
Sometimes impelling, force. None are aloof,
All succumb, till dumped at the saline strand,
Whence th'are rolled and dragged as rain from a roof.

The answer to a penetrating stare -
A spangled pearl in the turbulent sheen,
As chasing ripples project it here and there.
"Nature's tribe craves that even man be clean -
There is no call to cultivate and care,
Beauty prevails over all that has been."

The watery melodies sink to thought
While I rustle through interlocking growth.
Outstretched arms strive to grasp me, as if wrought
By a jealous maiden with whom a troth,
Has been broken. I remain uncaught,
Leaving the bower with lingering loth.

Now without th'all-sheltering canopy
And guardian growth, I can raise my gaze
To th'entombing heavens, partially free
From man's flaunting symbols, as essence rays
Pierce it to feed all actuality,
Before enforced to take a new-found phase.

People Are Strange

People are odd, people are strange,
Some of them must have become deranged.
Just listened to a bit of news,
Involved some clips and interviews,
Hostages, rebels and militants,
Children killed like tiny ants.

What in the world is occurring?
Violence and hatred recurring,
Slaughter for the sake of a cause,
Christians, lions, then Jaws.
Nothing much left, no moral law,
Political spins all flawed.

The Chechyens, the Muslims, the Jews,
Like chickens, turkeys and shrews,
Don't give a fig if you're stuck like a pig.
Some people are small, some people are big,
Some become the President,
It's a shame they're not more hesitant.

People are strange, people are weird,
Some are brave, and others are feared.
Don't know why those mines aren't cleared,
Don't know how that person was smeared.
We're all sheep waiting to be sheared,
Sailing a ship that can't be steered.

My Lord and my Master he drops me a clue,
Stakes me a claim in a new avenue.
There were women and men, children too,
Killed by those bastards who belong in a zoo,
Frittered and fluttered with no thought of you,
They'd have you boiled down to make some glue.

This fighting for peace it makes no sense,
In the name of religion's rabid pretence,
Disgust and revenge inspire the bereaved,
Mistrust of their motives fire the grieved.
People are nasty, people are strange,
Four eyes for an eye, nothing has changed.

A time may come when people realise,
To kill is to act like the Lord of the Flies,
To talk and to listen in the land of the wise.
It's of thinking like this we must agonise,
Be it speck or plank that's stuck in your eye,
Blindness to peace is what I despise.

Change only comes through the barrel of a gun,
Spine-chilling those words of Mao Tse Tung.
Mind-spinning the acts of Attila the Hun,
Have we learnt lessons from anyone?
History's been written by those who've won ....
People are strange I'll keep saying 'til I'm done ....

Slave Of Time

Just one more fag, one more beer,
One last thing to let me forget,
Just one more drag, one more dear?
It'll end in tears and deep regret.

Put off that time, staunch that fear,
Don't hold back, just push yourself,
It's not a crime to hold her near,
It's such a sin to be on the shelf.

Don't call time, don't ring that bell,
Leave us alone, I'd like one last chance,
Don't bring an end to all that went well,
I need her phone and maybe a dance.

Please don't shout "Time gentlemen please."
Please don't say "You've had too much mate."
I could climb a mountain, swing from the trees,
Don't starve my thirst, it may be too late.

These times are few, they're scant and they're rare,
A lady like this I usually miss.
One more beer please, if really you dare,
She'll have white wine, a kiss and a Bliss.

There are times like these when I could curse,
We've reached rapport, and beginning to giggle.
Now it's been stopped - we're in reverse,
No longer d'accord - impending niggle.

"Can I have your glasses please,"
"Haven't you got homes to go to?"
The thief called time begins to tease,
There's a fly in my ointment of flow too.

Just one more beer, and one more fag,
Try a curry, a pizza, a prance,
Trust me on this, and don't ever nag,
I'll show you I can snatch this chance.

"I'm sorry to say that I'm on my way,
I've got to get home before twelve."
I try to persuade her to stay,
The rest of it sticks twixt ourselves.

Once your labouring life's spent,
Dave Allen quipped once with a mock,
A retirement gift of ingenious intent,
Not silver, not gold, no, a carriage clock.

A Ravenous Dream

Ominous steel-billed, rook-like ravens
Invaded my slumbers last night.
They hopped and croaked as I sought havens,
Beady eyes flashing spells in the pale moonlight.

Van Gogh's swirling crows came to mind,
Portentous, perhaps, to the superstitious,
Frightening, maybe, in this world of the blind,
Craving carrion for morsels nutritious.

Was I to be spooked, spelled and eaten,
In a Hitchcock horror with eyes plucked out?
I resolved to resist, and not be beaten.
I caught one by his beak and chucked him out.

But, in this avine coven, they kept coming,
Chanting their caws and flexing their claws,
No mercy for me with the Sabbat beat drumming.
I wished they'd turn into jaunty jackdaws.

Bell, book and candle, tongue of toad,
Those witches' curses I tried to recall,
Nothing would make them hop back down the road,
Then my black cat arrived to disperse them all.

I woke in a sweat and mood of forewarning,
Black butcher-birds blinding my thoughts,
Gnawing away like rats 'til the morning,
I was sure that I'd erupt in weeping warts.

Not one for dreams, I wonder what it means?
Is it Satanic, Titanic and stuff like that?
Why was I plagued by these foul fiends?
Bemused, I purchased a black tom cat!

Sub-Dylanesque Blair-Sick Blues

Maggie was the P.M.
Juggled lives like Eminem,
A parliamentary blue gem,
All for her, none for them.
Fossil fuels under-sea,
Propped up economy.
Staged an Argie-bargie,
Grabbed those votes for all to see.
Look out Ma'am
Was anything planned?
God knows why not,
Soldiers got foot-rot,
Some were shot, others not.
We sank down the plug-hole,
Looked for jobs that she stole,
Ducked and bucked the dreaded dole.
Did Norman Tebbit have a soul?
No lives for paeons, plebs or proles.

Then came Johnny Major,
Grey man, no riot-rager,
Ate peas for tea I'll wager,
Said things that didn't faze ya.
Honest Johnny, unlike Ronnie
In his world of palimony,
No words of milk and honey,
Skipped out Deuteronomy.

Look out man
He's up to a scam,
Hatched a plot that went to pot,
Dropped the sword of Camelot.
They called him Maisy Daisy,
Workers labelled lazy,
Knew there was a way see,
To slip, slide and play free,
Swing the lead then blame me.

Johnny Major's embers,
Nothing to remember,
Chelsea, Surrey member,
Fearing Black September.
Iraqi grief beyond belief,
Famined world without relief,
Who's the victim? Who's the thief?
B.S.E. butchered beef.
Look out boy,
He had some new ploy,
Playing his trump card
Tried not to thump too hard,
Lost his friends, dropped his guard.
Wanna be metric, ban imperial yards.
The bull-ring of politics,
Maggie's bones, stones and sticks,
Magician with a box of tricks,
Left him screaming "It's a fix."

Up popped New Labour,
Yet another flavour,
Blair said he'd be like to Save ya,
And love to be your neighbour.
Fooled by many, not the few,
He spoke for he, not me, nor you,
Id and Ego grew and grew,
With his nouveau Tory crew.

Look out Sam
He's boiling up jam.
The Middle-East affray,
Some peace and love we'd pray,
Can't sit here, you can't stay,
Don't spill your beer, have feet of clay,
Keep your head down, come what may.
Beyond reproach he thinks he is,
Spinning for votes that he knows aren't his,
Best spark a strife like Suez.

Is Mike the one to save us?
Is he the man? Could you trust?
Needs a toupé, wants a truss,
Drives a coupé, it's got no rust,
A legal-beagle like all the rest,
His record worse than second best,
The also-rans have flown the nest,
Not caught on film getting dressed.
Look out Pom
They started with a bomb.
Allah he praised,
Why wasn't Baghdad razed?
Leave the crap to Tone and Jim,
Wait for George to phone him,
"It's tourists, not them Muslims."
Foreign policy gone squeaky,
Think-tanks have gotten leaky,
Mike's doctor's note got the vote - so very very freaky.

As I Recall

As I recall, I opened up my doors for you,
Opened up your eyes, your ears, your laughter too.
Saw Stoppard's "Rosencrantz and Guildenstern are dead."
Your grin gave birth, off'rin gemstones before I fled,
Manic and yellow, limp, lank, tonically bled.
Now I'll owe you nothing, not a cent, love instead.
As I recall, you opened up your gates for me,
Opened up my arms, palms, my heart, mystery's mis'ry.

Author's Comment

This poem was written in response to a challenge on a
poetry web site to write a piece including the words .....
calliope, guild, ring, candy, plankton, willow, fringe .....
these words are all contained within this piece.

Confusion's Confucius

Cool, callisthenic contortions gripping and grappling me;
Mind-bent, head-screwed visions upsetting me;
Can't work out left from right ... or my geometry.
Read some inspirational pieces today,
Won't use too many adjectives,
So I shall!
That's one of my prerogatives,
Good, sad, happy, mad, gay.
Nothing can usurp my inner plight - free me.

Small, synthetic socks sticking to my feet.
Sole-shrunk, soulless like little lost sheep,
Upon my tender toes they creep ....
Wrote poems of infinite prowess,
Even married that wondrous princess,
Lapsed to rhyme
And, in my mind, had great success
There's nothing like a lady's soft caress.
These thoughts so cataclysmic, caverned-deep.

Soothing, cooling, schooled, drooling musings.
I'm amused by this confusion, dump-trucked head accusing.
Booze-cruised mental fooling, fractual, fragmental footlings.
Got to grab a base-camp,
Stick envelope to stamp,
Now glue-gummed,
Kick that writer's creeping cramp,
Pour in the oil, luminate lamp,
Fire up the old juke-box, your Whirlitzer that zings.

Glorious the Magi Adoration, glad-happy nation's admiration.
No thoughts of consternation, crude gifts of
mental constipation.
No, no, no - NO! more bombs of pacifist persuasion.
Thought things of high times,
Lurid ladies' thigh lines.
Lost in space,
Looking for its mood sublime
Bemused by grot and grime
Lured myself back to a state of indignation.

Indian, isometric illusions illustrated my confusion,
Caused my mental contusion, conjured a creative diffusion.
No wit, no rhyme, no scheme, no profligative profusion.
A life of chasmic confusion,
That's my main conclusion,
That's it man!!!
I desire to paint allusions,
Aspire death's head delusion,
Cloying, clawing, stinking, scrawling seclusion.

Stuck to my word, eschewed adjectives, now the turn!
Beauteous, bounteous words fail to prevail that Grecian urn.
Inspirations sprung like sparkling shooting-stars unearned
Alliterative Al-anon,
Amblingly idling on
To a weird, benign beyond.
Didn't make plans,
Rolled scrolled stones, now long gone,
Sowed old, sad seeds of confusion.
Brigand bitches yearned bailey-bridges that I've burned,
The weasley worm has turned - I've lovingly learned
Love's lesson of clodded, clouded contusion.

Our Don

Everyone loves our Don,
As tough as biltong,
Moustached and oxen-strong,
Croaky voiced, craggy faced,
Down-to-earth, not straight-laced.
Today's Samaritan,
Uncle, Dad, a man's man.
Iron constitution,
Forthright resolution,
Honed hands like dinner-plates,
Husband and your best mate.
Treasure-pot of knowledge,
Never went to college,
Bar-fulcrum in The Plough,
Talks the thens to nows,
A barrack-room lawyer,
An ageing Tom Sawyer.
He's as strong as a tank,
And when we drunk he drank
Friends under the table,
Morrow comes he's able,
Willing, sturdy, stable,
Rock-steady, capable.
Aladdin's cave of tools,
He has no truck with fools,
He conducts his builder's schools,
Mentor and inventor,
Rarely an absentor.
Cricket fan through and through,
He knows me, you too!!
With smiling big broad grin
Generous to a sin.
Uncle Don, he's the one,
Loved by everyone.

Post Script

He showed him to the door
And said "Come back no more."
Fed up with the Scottish weasley law -
-Yer listened to some Paddy's pois'nous jaw,
Snow-fuelled nasal-voiced bile
Spewed with creepy smile
And cackle spawned in Hell.
Once that Monster's slithered up his arse
He'll realise the fucking farce
That Thief is trying to con
Just like he's done to ev'ryone
And then it's back to square one -
Bitching behind every back
List'ning to the very last one
Whose unkind words are lies
Are reared on shallow vapid lives,
Big Brothered, Big Sistered,
Get Me Outta Here - I'm a Non - entity.
Our Don will learn the sad old lesson,
Just like the rest of us - that Thief's a con,
Man of no morals, ethics, graces -
Who leaves nothing but slimey traces
In each and ev'ry place he's
Left his stinking verbal faeces.
Cometh the day, cometh Our Don
He'll spot his error and think on.
With fresh resolve and beard un-shorn
His house, leaving Thief forlorn,
Friendless, soulless, damned to Hell,
Ostracised, that ne'er-do-well,
Removed, the parasitic, putrid smell,
So Our Don can sit back relaxed,

And resignedly confess, somewhat taxed,
That the Mad Scotsman had it right,
Despite the powerful swelling pop-sight
In hind-sight realise the error of his ears,
His eyes, his nose, his intuition,
And execute an Inquisition
Just like Taucomada,
To make that Paddy "talk him harder",
Remove his trough-bound nose from larder,
And speak the Truth that, to him's,
Anathema, alien, a Satanic hymn.
Once the Truth is out there'll be no doubt
That scratched slates _can_ be scoured,
Wiped clean - 'umble pie can be devoured
And status quo with apologies showered
To rekindle a loving friendship,
Shattered by a bog-trotting shit,
Foolish Pride swallowed
To benefit the Hallowed.
And old dog _can_ learn new tricks,
Although it makes him sick,
He's wise enough to know
That love is white-blinded in the snow,
And errors are made to Learn
If bridges have been burned,
Or dreams shattered that once were yearned.
Enlightenment achieved,
Our Don will be believed
Once more - after the flood,
After the tsunami-spilling blood,
The Thief returned to mud.
God bless Our Don,
Fallible - just like ev'ryone.

Lorna, Lorna Lovely

Lorna, Lorna, lovely
A girl up 'til three
Lorna, Lorna, lovely
A pride and joy to me
Lorna, Lorna, lovely
Lady now – no baby
Lorna, Lorna, lovely
Not one who says "maybe"
Lorna, Lorna, lovely
Hair fair, once curly
Lorna, Lorna, lovely
Amidst the hurly-burly
Lorna, Lorna, lovely
Frivolous and free
Lorna, Lorna, lovely
Consume the world with glee
Lorna, Lorna, lovely
You'd sleep upon my knee
Lorna, Lorna, lovely
Like me, you can't agree
Lorna, Lorna, lovely
Spirit-ful – not twee
Lorna, Lorna, lovely
Take your chances gladly
Lorna, Lorna, lovely
The world behaves quite madly
Lorna, Lorna, lovely
You have great personality

Lorna, Lorna, lovely
Mum and me we love you see
Lorna, Lorna, lovely
Your life shall be sweet and juicy
Lorna, Lorna, lovely
On this your 18th anniversary
Lorna, Lorna, lovely
Live long, love life, crack open the bubbly!

Lorna – Age 18

Little Lorns you're eighteen today
No more borrowed IDs, or "bunking off of school".
It seems yesterday in Mum's heels you'd play
Hand-ear, thumb-mouth, "Dad's so cruel".
A girl with spirit so free, no shrinking rose she,
Curly locks flowing, 'til that Hottentot!
Went to the Dressers, with a stinking cold me,
Mum's blood got a clot, "did she like it?", not a lot!
So you vented your revenge on one of your friends,
Cropped her hair in a folly, as on one of your dollies.
It's a history that won't ever end
"I'm a veggie by golly, and I love lolly".
Dear Ferret times change in this world of alarm,
Darling girl you're a delight, a rascal with charm.
I'll always be a doting, balding Father to you
You're a star to me, no matter what you do.
I'm proud as your Dad, and Mum's as proud too,
We're both as glad, your future's your oyster, down to you.

My Son James

He's kind of heart and sound of mind
I'm so proud he's a son of mine
He's sharp of wit and full of mirth
It's been this way since his teenage birth.
Thank the Lord he's hale and healthy
In magnetic charm he's wealthy.
I'm so proud he's my lovely lad,
He's himself, my boy, and I'm glad.
He's caring, considerate, calm,
He carefully causes no harm.
Not sporty, not spiteful nor crude,
Bolshy, belligerent nor rude,
Doesn't drink beer, spirits nor wine,
I'm so proud he's a son of mine.
I'm so proud he's my lovely lad,
He's himself, my boy, and I'm glad.
He rolls the philosopher's stone
Speaks quietly when on the phone
He picks all the shit from the bull
Keeps his mouth tight-shut when it's full.
There's no mountain that he won't climb
I'm so proud he's a son of mine.
I'm so proud he's my lovely lad,
He's himself, my boy, and I'm glad.
I'm so proud he's a son of mine,
His brain is so sharp it's sublime,
If pushed he'll catch you out quickly,
If rushed, spreads his bread thickly,
Tell you that everything's fine,
Walk you down the finest of lines.
I'm so proud he's my lovely lad,
He's himself, my boy, and I'm glad.

He can spot a nail from a screw
Ridicules the old and the new,
I'm so proud he's a son of mine.
The Satanic pearls divine
He fast-casts like lemming 'fore swine
Off a cliff we've never defined.
I'm so proud he's my lovely lad,
He's himself, my boy, and I'm glad.

Once he was quiet, blonde and thin,
Now bright-spark with thickest of skin.
His shoes, like mine, are seldom shined,
I'm so proud he's a son of mine.
He'll tell you the truth with a grin,
Observe all your faults and your sin.
Never low-down sad, only bold
He makes me smile as I grow old.

Lightning Source UK Ltd.
Milton Keynes UK
UKOW04f2053030714

234513UK00002B/23/P